Macmillan/McGraw-Hill Science

EARTH
BENEATH
YOUR
FEET

AUTHORS

Mary Atwater
The University of Georgia

Prentice Baptiste
University of Houston

Lucy Daniel
Rutherford County Schools

Jay Hackett
University of Northern Colorado

Richard Moyer
University of Michigan, Dearborn

Carol Takemoto
Los Angeles Unified School District

Nancy Wilson
Sacramento Unified School District

A volcano erupting

Macmillan/McGraw-Hill School Publishing Company
New York Chicago Columbus

MACMILLAN / McGRAW-HILL

SCIENCE TURNS MINDS ON ™

CONSULTANTS

Assessment:

Janice M. Camplin
Curriculum Coordinator, Elementary Science
Mentor, Western New York
Lake Shore Central Schools
Angola, NY

Mary Hamm
Associate Professor
Department of Elementary Education
San Francisco State University
San Francisco, CA

Cognitive Development:

Dr. Elisabeth Charron
Assistant Professor of Science Education
Montana State University
Bozeman, MT

Sue Teele
Director of Education Extension
University of California, Riverside
Riverside, CA

Cooperative Learning:

Harold Pratt
Executive Director of Curriculum
Jefferson County Public Schools
Golden, CO

Earth Science:

Thomas A. Davies
Research Scientist
The University of Texas
Austin, TX

David G. Futch
Associate Professor of Biology
San Diego State University
San Diego, CA

Dr. Shadia Rifai Habbal
Harvard-Smithsonian Center for Astrophysics
Cambridge, MA

Tom Murphree, Ph.D.
Global Systems Studies
Monterey, CA

Suzanne O'Connell
Assistant Professor
Wesleyan University
Middletown, CT

Environmental Education:

Cheryl Charles, Ph.D.
Executive Director
Project Wild
Boulder, CO

Gifted:

Sandra N. Kaplan
Associate Director, National/State Leadership
Training Institute on the Gifted/Talented
Ventura County Superintendent of Schools Office
Northridge, CA

Global Education:

M. Eugene Gilliom
Professor of Social Studies and Global Education
The Ohio State University
Columbus, OH

Merry M. Merryfield
Assistant Professor of Social Studies and Global
Education
The Ohio State University
Columbus, OH

Intermediate Specialist

Sharon L. Strating
Missouri State Teacher of the Year
Northwest Missouri State University
Marysville, MO

Life Science:

Carl D. Barrentine
Associate Professor of Biology
California State University
Bakersfield, CA

V.L. Holland
Professor and Chair, Biological Sciences
Department
California Polytechnic State University
San Luis Obispo, CA

Donald C. Lisowy
Education Specialist
New York, NY

Dan B. Walker
Associate Dean for Science Education and
Professor of Biology
San Jose State University
San Jose, CA

Literature:

Dr. Donna E. Norton
Texas A&M University
College Station, TX

Tina Thoburn, Ed.D.
President
Thoburn Educational Enterprises, Inc.
Ligonier, PA

Macmillan/McGraw-Hill School Division
10 Union Square East
New York, New York 10003

Printed in the United States of America

ISBN 0-02-274262-X / 3

4 5 6 7 8 9 VHJ 99 98 97 96 95 94 93

A Himalayan mountain peak

Mathematics:

Martin L. Johnson
Professor, Mathematics Education
University of Maryland at College Park
College Park, MD

Physical Science:

Max Diem, Ph.D.
Professor of Chemistry
City University of New York, Hunter College
New York, NY

Gretchen M. Gillis
Geologist
Maxus Exploration Company
Dallas, TX

Wendell H. Potter
Associate Professor of Physics
Department of Physics
University of California, Davis
Davis, CA

Claudia K. Viehland
Educational Consultant, Chemist
Sigma Chemical Company
St. Louis, MO

Reading:

Jean Wallace Gillet
Reading Teacher
Charlottesville Public Schools
Charlottesville, VA

Charles Temple, Ph. D.
Associate Professor of Education
Hobart and William Smith Colleges
Geneva, NY

Safety:

Janice Sutkus
Program Manager: Education

National Safety Council
Chicago, IL

Science Technology and Society (STS):

William C. Kyle, Jr.
Director, School Mathematics and Science Center
Purdue University
West Lafayette, IN

Social Studies:

Mary A. McFarland
Instructional Coordinator of
Social Studies, K-12, and
Director of Staff Development
Parkway School District
St. Louis, MO

Students Acquiring English:

Mrs. Bronwyn G. Frederick, M.A.
Bilingual Teacher
Pomona Unified School District
Pomona, CA

Misconceptions:

Dr. Charles W. Anderson
Michigan State University
East Lansing, MI

Dr. Edward L. Smith
Michigan State University
East Lansing, MI

Multicultural:

Bernard L. Charles
Senior Vice President
Quality Education for Minorities Network
Washington, DC

Cheryl Willis Hudson
Graphic Designer and Publishing Consultant
Part Owner and Publisher, Just Us Books, Inc.
Orange, NJ

Paul B. Janeczko
Poet
Hebron, MA

James R. Murphy
Math Teacher
La Guardia High School
New York, NY

Ramon L. Santiago
Professor of Education and Director of ESL
Lehman College, City University of New York
Bronx, NY

Clifford E. Trafzer
Professor and Chair, Ethnic Studies
University of California, Riverside
Riverside, CA

STUDENT ACTIVITY TESTERS

Jennifer Kildow
Brooke Straub
Cassie Zistl
Betsy McKeown
Seth McLaughlin
Max Berry
Wayne Henderson

FIELD TEST TEACHERS

Sharon Ervin
San Pablo Elementary School
Jacksonville, FL

Michelle Gallaway
Indianapolis Public School #44
Indianapolis, IN

Kathryn Gallman
#7 School
Rochester, NY

Karla McBride
#44 School
Rochester, NY

Diane Pease
Leopold Elementary
Madison, WI

Kathy Perez
Martin Luther King Elementary
Jacksonville, FL

Ralph Stamler
Thoreau School
Madison, WI

Joanne Stern
Hilltop Elementary School
Glen Burnie, MD

Janet Young
Indianapolis Public School #90
Indianapolis, IN

CONTRIBUTING WRITER

Nancy Nielsen

Earth Beneath Your Feet

Lessons   **Themes**

Unit Introduction **Earth Beneath Your Feet** ....Patterns of Change 6

Rocks may be a part of your everyday life, but how much do you know about the rocks right under your feet?

1 What's Inside a Rock ? ....Scale and Structure 12

Rocks—You walk on them, you skip them, but do you know what's inside them?

2 How Do Rocks Change ? ....Patterns of Change 26

Where did all the soil come from? Could it have come from rocks?

3 How Do Rocks Form? .... Patterns of Change 36

Learn how Earth makes rocks in this close-up look at the "rock factory."

4 How Does Land Form and Change ? ....Evolution...............48

Don't look now, but the ground is changing! Find out what's happening to landforms all over Earth.

Unit Wrap Up What Else Is Beneath Your Feet? ....Patterns of Change 60

If you ever thought of digging a hole down through Earth, don't start until you've read this!

Activities!

EXPLORE

What Are Rocks Made Of? *14*

Powerful Water *28*

Rocks Under Pressure! *38*

Water Power! *50*

TRY THIS

Rock Collection *7*

The Scratch Test *18*

True Colors *20*

Smooth Out the Rough Edges *31*

Rock Salad Dressing *32*

Where does the Rock Go? *33*

Has Your Neighborhood Weathered? *34*

Rock-in-a-Cup *43*

Is Your School Yard Changing? *58*

Learning From a Rock *63*

Features

Links

Literature Links

Science in Literature **10**

Everybody Needs a Rock **17**

Could You Ever? Dig a Hole to China **61**

Music/Art Link

Modeling Clay **24**

Math Link

Weather Adds Up...**30**

Social Studies Link

Built To Last **46**

Language Arts Link

Legends..**52**

Jewelry Maker...**41**

Focus on Environment

Asbestos..**25**

Polluting Rocks **35**

Focus on Technology

Measuring Mountains and Molehills **55**

Departments

Glossary..**64**

Index **66**

Credits **68**

Earth Beneath Your Feet

When you're outside playing, what do you think is beneath your feet? The ground underneath you is made of many, many things. If you could take away the grass and soil, what would you find? Whether you're on a mountain, in a valley, or in a field, rocks are under everything.

Half Dome in Yosemite National Park, California

You have probably seen rocks before. In a stream, in the soil, and in the park—you can find rocks almost anywhere.

Rocks have been around for a long time. You may have heard of the saying, "It's as hard as a rock." But how hard are rocks? Are they so hard that they never change? Do sidewalks ever change? Have mountains always been the same as they are now?

TRY THIS

Activity!

Rock Collection

What You Need

5 rocks, 1 polished rock, *Activity Log* page 1

Collect five rocks. Clean them if they are dirty. Line up your rocks and number them 1–5. On a chart in your *Activity Log,* mark which are large, small, smooth, rough, shiny, and dull. Compare your results with another group. Look at the polished rock. How is it different from the rocks you picked off the ground? What do you think made it that way?

Rocks fascinated people who lived long ago. People who lived during the Stone Age used rocks as tools. They fit rocks to pieces of wood to make hammers. They chipped rocks to make knives and points for spears. They also struck pieces of flint and rocks containing iron together to make a spark for the fires they used to cook and keep warm.

Centuries ago, African people, especially those in northern areas such as Nigeria (nī jîr´ ē ə) and Ethiopia (ē´thē ō´ pē ə), made figures out of bronze, gold, and other metals. They were also good at rock painting and pottery making.

Ancient tools made from stone

The longest wall ever built is the Great Wall of China. It is almost 6,400 kilometers (4,000 miles) long. It is made of rocks, bricks, and soil. The wall was built to protect China from invaders. It took hundreds of years to build.

*Bushman paintings
in South Africa*

The ancient Egyptians (i jip´ shənz) built pyramids out of rocks. They were tombs for important people. About 80 pyramids are still standing in Egypt.

The Anasazi (ä´na sä´ zē) were a group of Native Americans who lived in southwestern Colorado about 1,000 years ago. They were called cliff-dwellers because they built whole towns in rock cliffs. Their rock homes had bedrooms, living rooms, corn-grinding rooms, storage rooms, and rooms used for religious meetings.

Over the next few weeks, you'll explore what rocks are, what makes them different, and what people do with them.

Science in Literature

Many people explore wild and exotic places on this planet. They dive deep into the oceans to learn about what lives there. Some people even look out into space to find out what's out there. But the ground right beneath your feet can be just as interesting. To help you begin exploring the world under your feet, read some of these books. Books can be as valuable to a scientist as a magnifying glass or a telescope.

Aladdin Books

EVERYBODY NEEDS A ROCK

by BYRD BAYLOR with pictures by PETER PARNALL

Everybody Needs A Rock by Byrd Baylor. New York: Aladdin, 1974.

You may think all rocks are the same. In this book, Baylor gives you ten rules for finding your own special rock. Read this book and begin a rock collection with your very special rock.

COULD YOU EVER?
Dig a Hole to China
Dr. David Darling

Could You Ever? Dig a Hole to China by Dr. David Darling. Minneapolis: Dillon/ Macmillan, 1990.

How deep can you dig a hole? In this book Darling explores what you might encounter if you had an entire year to dig a hole as deep as you could. As you read this book, try to imagine what you might find if you started to dig a hole in your own backyard!

Other Good Books To Read

The Sun, the Wind and the Rain by Lisa Westberg Peters. New York: Henry Holt, 1988.

If you have ever built a mountain out of sand, you'll enjoy learning how a real mountain is formed. How long does it last? This book compares what happens to a mountain Elizabeth builds to one built by Earth processes.

The Big Rock by Bruce Hiscock. New York: Atheneum, 1988.

Does a rock always stay the same? Read about a rock's life in the Adirondack Mountains in New York.

Geography From A to Z by Jack Knowlton. New York: Thomas Y. Crowell, 1988.

Colorful pictures of landforms will teach you everything you've wanted to know about Earth's features.

11

What's Inside a Rock?

Rocks and things made of rocks are all around you. There are thousands of different rocks. But what are rocks made of? What makes some rocks colorful? What makes some rocks hard?

Digging for rocks

A bridge made from rocks

A statue made from a rock

Many buildings are made from rocks.

Every day you probably see ways people use rocks. You see stone bridges, statues, and buildings. The sidewalks you walk on have rocks in them. The streets you came to school on may have been made from them. Gravel roads and driveways are another place you can find rocks.

You know several things that are made from rocks. But do you know what rocks are made of?

Activity!

What Are Rocks Made Of?

Have you ever looked closely at a rock? What is it made of? In this activity, you will explore several rocks to try to find out what they're made of.

What You Need

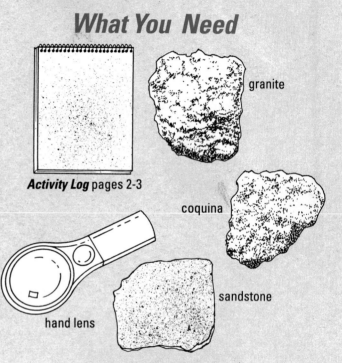

Activity Log pages 2-3

granite

coquina

sandstone

5 rocks you collected

hand lens

What To Do

1 Touch each rock. How does it feel? Write your observations in your *Activity Log.*

2 Smell each rock. Record your observations in your *Activity Log.*

3 Look at each rock. Write down what color it is. Are there any lines or patterns in any of the rocks?

4 Predict what you think each rock is made of. Record your prediction in your *Activity Log.*

5 Use the hand lens to look at each rock again.

6 Write down the parts you see that you didn't see before.

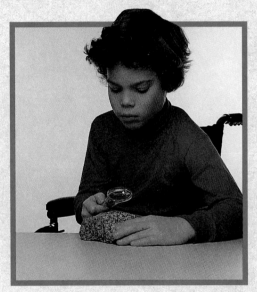

What Happened?

1. Did any rocks feel the same? Did any smell the same? Did any have the same color?
2. When you looked under the magnifying glass, did any of the rocks look the same?

What Now?

1. Did you think any of the rocks were made of the same thing?
2. What do you think the rocks were made of?

EXPLORE

15

Rocks Are Made of Minerals

In the Explore Activity, you saw that rocks are different. You also saw that some rocks are made of smaller parts. Some rocks are made of many different things.

Some of the things you saw in the rocks were minerals (min´ ər əlz). **Minerals** are solids that form naturally. They are not plants or animals. Minerals make a rock look and feel the way it does. They give rocks their different colors. They also make the rock hard or soft.

The mineral mica

The mineral feldspar

Everybody Needs A Rock

What kind of rocks do you like? If you were to look for a special rock, what color would it be? What would it smell and feel like? What shape would you look for? The things you like about rocks depend on the minerals the rocks are made of. In *Everybody Needs A Rock*, you will find out how to search for the rock you like best. Read it and then use the rules to find a rock. Write in your *Activity Log* on page 4 what you like most about your rock.

The mineral quartz

There are more than 3,000 kinds of minerals. They have different colors, hardnesses, and crystal shapes. Minerals are different because they are made of different materials. And they have their own structure inside. These are **properties** of minerals.

Where do you find minerals? Minerals can be found in rocks all around you. They are also found in the soil and in water. Minerals are even in plants and animals. You may eat a cereal with minerals added to it for breakfast. Living things need minerals to live and grow.

A granite rock

17

The Properties of Minerals

Let's look at some minerals and their properties that make them different.

Quartz (kwôrtz) and rock salt are two very common minerals. Rock salt, or halite (hal´ īt), is the same as table salt. It is often found in rocks where ancient seas once were. Quartz is found in granite and is the most common mineral in the sand you find at the beach.

TRY THIS

Activity!

The Scratch Test

What You Need

nail, rock salt, quartz, *Activity Log* page 5

Look at the two minerals. Record your observations in your *Activity Log.* Take the nail and carefully try to scratch the quartz. Look for a scratch mark. Try to scratch the salt with the nail. Look for a scratch mark in the salt. Which mineral was harder? How do you know?

Sand used for sandblasting

Hardness

You can tell how hard something is by seeing what scratches it. The nail you used in the activity could scratch the salt but not the quartz. This means that the quartz was harder than the salt. Some minerals, like diamonds, are very hard. Other minerals, like talc (talk) and graphite (graf´ īt), are so soft your fingernail can scratch them!

The hardness of a mineral is important in how it's used. Would it be better to use quartz or rock salt in sandpaper? Which do you think would last longer?

In sandblasting, sand is blown at very high speeds. The hard minerals wear away metal and rocks. Why do you think this worker needs protective clothing?

Minds On! During the gold rush in California, miners searched for gold. They needed to be able to tell real gold from another mineral, pyrite (pī′ rīt). To tell them apart, the miners would bite the mineral they found. If they saw a bite mark in the mineral, they knew it was real gold. What property were they testing? ●

19

Color and Shine

Minerals can look very different. Some are pink and dull. Some are gold and shiny. You can't always trust your eyes, though. Water and air can change the color of some minerals.

To see the true color of a mineral, you can rub it on a tile.

The streak color always stays the same. This is why people use this test to help identify minerals.

Activity!

True Colors

What You Need

unglazed white ceramic tile, mineral samples, *Activity Log* **page 6**

How different are the color and shine of minerals? In your *Activity Log,* record your observations of each mineral. Which minerals are shiny or look like metal? Rub each sample once across the tile and blow off the extra powder. Record the color of the streak left on the tile. Was the streak color always the same as the color of the mineral? Did all the minerals have the same streak colors?

Malachite

Hematite

Galena

Breaking

You may have noticed as you've looked at minerals that they have different shapes. This is because minerals break in different ways. Some minerals break leaving a flat side. Other minerals break into different shapes. Some minerals may break in several directions.

The way minerals break is very important in how we use them. Diamonds are broken in certain ways that make them beautiful for jewelry. The diamond on the left is what they look like naturally. Next to it is what they look like after they're broken. Diamonds are only found in a few places in the world. Most of them are in South Africa, but there are also some in India and South America.

How We Use Minerals

The minerals that make up rocks can be very useful. How we use the minerals depends on their properties.

The mineral graphite is soft. This makes it a perfect choice for what you use it for almost every day. The black stuff in your pencil is made of graphite. Because it's soft, it will rub off on your paper as you write. The line you draw on your paper is the true color of the graphite.

Diamonds are also used for other things besides jewelry. Diamonds are the hardest of all minerals. This makes them good for drilling or cutting other hard materials such as rocks. Drill bits are coated with diamond dust. This makes them able to drill through very hard rock.

Calcite (kal´ sīt) is a mineral found in chalk. It's almost as soft as graphite, so it is good for writing on chalkboards and sidewalks. It also has a clear streak color. This makes it easy to make colored chalk.

Clay is a group of minerals that are very useful. There are different kinds of clay, found in many places. When it is moist, it is very soft and people mold and shape it into pottery and bricks. Baking it, though, makes it very hard.

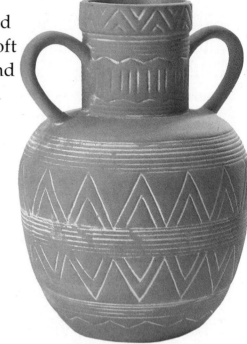
Pottery made from clay

Clay as it is found in the ground

Modeling Clay

Clay has been used by artists for a long time. Ancient groups of people in all parts of the world made pottery. The Greeks and Egyptians were very skilled at making pottery. Very old Chinese pots and vases are considered master works of art.

Many artists make sculptures out of clay. Try making a sculpture using some modeling clay. Do you think the clay mineral is hard or soft?

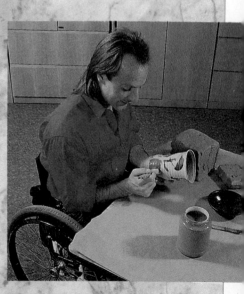
An artist making pottery.

S C I E N C E **TECHNOLOGY** **AND** **Society** **F**ocus **on E**nvironment *Asbestos*

Sometimes, the minerals we use are harmful to us. **Asbestos** (as bes´ təs) is a grayish-white mineral that can cause a lot of health problems. Because it doesn't burn, it was used in ceilings for fire protection. Scientists now know that when asbestos comes loose and floats in the air, it can be harmful. Because of this, it is being carefully removed from many buildings. Asbestos removal is very expensive because of the safety measures needed to protect the workers.

Asbestos fibers

Sum It Up

It's easy to mix up rocks and minerals. Just like a salad is made of many vegetables, a rock is made of many minerals. The minerals that are in a rock have many different properties. Some are hard and some are soft. Some are black and some are clear. Rocks are different because of the different minerals they have in them.

Critical Thinking

1. How do rocks and minerals differ?
2. How would things be different if there were no minerals on Earth?
3. What would rocks be like if all minerals on Earth were the same?

How Do Rocks Change?

Have you ever looked at an old, rusted car and wondered what it looked like when it was new? You've probably never wondered that about a rock, but you should think about it! When you pick up a rock, chances are it looks very differently than it did 1,000 years ago.

The ruins of Great Zimbabwe

An old tombstone

A stone wall crumbling

Plants breaking apart a sidewalk

In southern Africa there is an ancient settlement called Great Zimbabwe (zim bäb´ wē). All that's left are many stone walls built on a hill and in a valley.

Over the years, the walls have changed. The stones have worn, and some of them have fallen apart. It doesn't look the same today as it looked 500 years ago.

Minds On! You don't have to travel all the way to Zimbabwe, though, to see rocks that have changed. Look at old tombstones in a cemetery. Can you find a crumbling stone wall or sidewalk in your neighborhood? How have they changed? In this lesson you will explore what changes rocks. ●

Activity!

Powerful Water

Most people probably think that water is not very powerful. Think of an ice cube. Could it split a rock in half? In this activity you will make a model that will explore this question.

What You Need

Activity Log pages 7-8

dough mixture

water

freezer

small balloon

waxed paper

What To Do

1 Fill the balloon with water until it is about the size of a golf ball. Tie the end so there is no air inside the balloon.

2 On waxed paper, flatten a 5-cm ball of the dough mixture. Press it until it is 1/2 cm thick.

3 Carefully wrap the dough around the balloon. Make sure none of the balloon shows through the dough. Smooth the dough so there are no cracks.

4 Set your "rock" on waxed paper and let it harden for two or three days.

5 After it's dry, place it in a freezer overnight.

6 Record your observations in your *Activity Log.*

What Happened?

1. What happened to your "rock?"
2. What did the water inside the balloon do?

What Now?

1. How could what happened to your "rock" happen to real rocks?
2. How does this compare to a sidewalk or a street breaking apart?

Change by Wind, Rain, and Ice

In the Explore Activity, you saw one way rocks can change. When it rains, water gets into cracks that are in rocks. As the water freezes, it needs more space. The ice pushes the rock apart. Ice really can be powerful!

But it doesn't have to be cold for rocks to change. Rocks are changed in deserts, swamps, and arctic mountains. However, the way they change is very different.

Climates have an effect on how fast rocks change. Cleopatra's Needle (klē ə pa´ traz • nē´ dəl) is a 3,000-year-old stone monument that was moved from Egypt to New York City in 1881. It has changed much faster because of its new climate.

Cleopatra's Needle in New York

Cleopatra's Needle in Cairo, Egypt

Math Link
Weather Adds Up

Look at the table and compare the climates of Cairo and New York City. On page 9 in your *Activity Log*, record the difference in winter temperatures between the two places. Which city has the greater rainfall? What do you think caused the monument to weather faster in New York City?

	New York	Cairo
Average Temperature in Winter	– 6° C (21° F)	13° C (56° F)
Rainfall Per Year	99 cm (39 in)	0-10 cm (0-4 in)

Activity! *Smooth Out the Rough Edges*

What You Need

plastic jar with lid, 2 pieces of chalk, water,
Activity Log **page 10**

Water changes rocks in more ways than just freezing. How does moving water change rocks? Fill the jar half full of water. Break each piece of chalk into three pieces. Put all the pieces of chalk, except one, into the jar, and put the lid on. Take turns shaking the jar for 5 min. Take out the pieces of chalk and compare them to the piece that was left out. Record your observations in your *Activity Log.* Compare the chalk to the polished rock you observed in the Try This Activity on page 7. How do you think this rock was polished?

Moving water can do the same thing to rocks that it did to the pieces of chalk. In a stream, the rocks bump into each other. This breaks away sharp edges, making them round and smooth.

Because there's no water, wind changes desert rocks. The wind blows sand across the rocks, slowly "sanding" it away.

When wind, water, or ice breaks rock into smaller pieces, it is called **weathering** (we<u>th</u>´ ər ing). The pieces that are broken off don't just stay where they are, though. Either they fall, or wind, water, or ice carries them away. When this happens, it is called **erosion** (i rō´ zhən).

31

Chemical Weathering

Rocks can be changed by things other than water, wind, and ice. When the substances that minerals are made of change, it is called **chemical weathering** (kem´ i kəl • we<u>th</u>´ ər ing). Things that are in the air, soil, plants, and water cause the chemical weathering of rocks. To see this happen, do this next activity.

TRY THIS **Activity!** *Rock Salad Dressing*

What You Need

apron, goggles, vinegar, clear plastic jar, 1 piece of chalk, *Activity Log* page 11

Vinegar, a common part of salad dressing, can also chemically weather rocks! *Safety Tip:* Wear an apron and goggles. Be careful not to spill the vinegar, and keep your face away from the jar. Put a chalk piece in the jar. Cover the chalk with vinegar. Record or draw your observations in your *Activity Log.*

Chemical weathering usually happens much slower than in the Try This Activity. The chemicals normally found in water and air are weaker and weather the minerals more slowly.

Sometimes the minerals in rocks will be chemically weathered by dissolving. When a mineral **dissolves** (di zolvz´), it mixes with the liquid it's in. The liquid then carries it away.

When minerals slowly dissolve, caves can form. The minerals are carried away leaving a large space.

Where Do the Pieces Go?

All these different ways of weathering break up rocks into smaller and smaller pieces. But what happens to the pieces? Where do they go? To explore this question, do the next Try This Activity.

Rocks are weathered by water, wind, ice, and chemicals until the pieces are very tiny.

TRY THIS

Activity!

Where Does the Rock Go?

What You Need

small spoonful of soil from outside, 2 pieces of sandstone, 2 pieces of white paper, hand lens, *Activity Log* page 12

Over a piece of paper, gently rub the rocks together. Carefully spread the spoonful of soil on the other piece of paper. Break up any large chunks of soil. Use the hand lens to examine both the soil and the material that came off the rocks. How are the pieces that rubbed off the sandstone like the soil? How are they different?

These pieces get mixed with the remains of dead plants and animals to make soil.

As a part of the soil, the minerals from the rocks are used by plants and animals. They need the minerals to live and grow.

You may see pebbles and rocks of different sizes in a pile of dirt. But the very tiny pieces of sand were once rocks, too. **Soil** is a combination of minerals, dead plants and animals, water, and air.

Weathering Changes Your World

There are many things around you that are changed by weathering. Not only are rocks changed by it, but things made from rocks and minerals are also changed.

TRY THIS

Activity!

Has Your Neighborhood Weathered?

What You Need

Activity Log page 13

What have you seen that has been weathered? With an adult, go outside and find out. Look for signs of weathering. Look at buildings. Look at streets. Look at sidewalks. List everything you see in your *Activity Log.* What caused the weathering? Was it water, wind, ice, or plants? Was it chemicals?

Much of the construction on roads that you see is to repair damage done by weathering.

Maybe you saw some potholes in the street. Weathering causes potholes to form. Just like ice broke the "rock" in the Explore Activity on page 28, ice breaks roads making potholes.

Sidewalks can form cracks and crumble in this way, too. But you can also see how plants change things.

This sidewalk is breaking apart as the roots of the tree grow larger.

SCIENCE TECHNOLOGY AND Society **F**ocus **on E**nvironment

Polluting Rocks

Cars and factories pollute the air and water with substances that can cause chemical weathering. This is a problem for buildings, statues, and other things made from rocks. Pollution speeds up the weathering of these things.

Fixing damage done to rocks by pollution is expensive. In the United States, cleaning and repairing statues and buildings harmed by chemical weathering from pollution costs several billion dollars every year.

Sum It Up

Although rocks appear as if they could last forever, they can be changed. Weathering by water, wind, ice, and plants changes rocks and minerals. Weathering is the powerful process of change that makes rocks and minerals become part of the soil.

Critical Thinking

1. What causes rocks near rivers to be smooth?

2. Where do the minerals that plants use come from?

3. What would Earth be like if rocks did not weather? How would sidewalks, buildings, and roads in your neighborhood be different?

How Do Rocks Form?

Although you can't tell it, rocks underneath you are changing right now. The ground beneath your feet and beneath the oceans is a busy "rock factory." Rocks are made and rocks are broken down. How does this factory work?

Monument Valley

A volcano

Sandstone

Gneiss

The changes that happen to rocks take many years. It may seem very slow, but there is a lot going on. Some rocks are being made. Other rocks are being broken down. Rocks are being changed into different rocks. Rocks are being buried under layers of new rocks.

Minds On! Changes occur all around you every day, even though you might not notice them. Name three things that change in a short time. Name three things that change over a long time. On page 14 in your *Activity Log,* put these changes in order from slowest to fastest. ●

Activity!

Rocks Under Pressure!

You know that rocks are made of different minerals, but how do they get put together to make a rock? In this activity you will use clay to make a model of a rock that is formed by heat and pressure.

What You Need

Activity Log pages 15-16

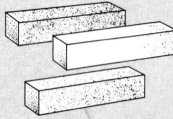

3 colors of modeling clay

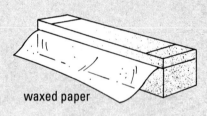

waxed paper

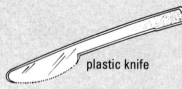

plastic knife

What To Do

1 Make several small balls from each color of clay.

2 Gently stick different-colored balls together to make a larger ball.

Safety!

See *Safety Tip* in step 4.

3 On a piece of waxed paper, press down the ball until it is flat. Turn the flattened ball on its edge and press down again.

4 Cut your "rock" in half with the plastic knife. *Safety Tip:* Use the knife carefully.

5 Draw what the inside of your "rock" looks like in your *Activity Log.*

What Happened?

1. How did the shape of the small, colored balls change?
2. What effect did pressure from your hands have on the shape of the small balls?

What Now?

1. Look at your "rock." Would it be easier to separate the colored balls now, or before you pressed the rock together?
2. How could heat help change the clay?

Igneous Rocks

In the Explore Activity, you explored one process that forms rocks. You saw that pressure from your hands changed the shape of the clay balls. The "rock" you ended up with looked much different from when you started.

Just like this, the rocks underneath you have been changed from one kind to another. Some are melted. Some are changed by pressure and heat like the clay was. Others are made when pieces of weathered rocks become stuck together.

Lava cools quickly.

One place you can see rocks being made is near a volcano. The lava is melted rock material that comes from deep inside Earth. It oozes or erupts through cracks in Earth's surface. As it cools, it forms rocks.

40

Rocks formed from the cooling of melted material are **igneous** (igʹ nē əs) rocks. There are many kinds of igneous rocks. They are different in a couple of ways. One way is that different igneous rocks have different amounts or kinds of minerals in them.

How fast or how slow the rock cools is another difference. Melted rock material can cool slowly, deep inside Earth. It can also cool quickly on the surface of Earth. When rocks cool slowly, large crystals form. **Crystals** (krisʹ təlz) are a repeating pattern of particles. Particles are the very small pieces that minerals are made of. When a rock cools quickly, the crystals don't get large enough to see.

Mineral crystals

Granite (granʹ it)

Obsidian (ob sidʹ ē ən) is an igneous rock that can be made of the same minerals as granite. Obsidian is different because it forms by cooling quickly. Native Americans used this glassy rock to make knives and spear points.

CAREERS

Jewelry Maker

Valerie Miller is a jewelry maker. She likes to look for igneous rocks. One thing you can find among igneous rocks is crystals. She uses different sizes and colors of crystals she finds to make all kinds of jewelry.

Valerie learned how to find crystals by studying about rocks and how they form. After many years of experience, she finds plenty of crystals for her jewelry.

Sedimentary Rocks

The cooling of melted rocks is only one way rocks are formed. Do you remember how rocks break and change from weathering and erosion? Small pieces of rocks and minerals can become stuck together to form another kind of rock. This is called a **sedimentary** (sed´ ə mən´ tə rē) rock. They are made of rock and mineral pieces, and remains of plants and animals. The pieces are stuck together by other minerals.

The White Cliffs of Dover in England are made of a sedimentary rock called chalk. Chalk is a kind of limestone (līm´ stōn´). It's made of the mineral calcite and very tiny animals that once lived in oceans.

Another sedimentary rock, coquina (kō kē´ nə), is made of sand and pieces of shells.

Activity! *Rock-in-a-Cup*

What You Need

2 paper cups, spoon, sand, small gravel, sugar, water, *Activity Log* page 17

You can make your own model of a sedimentary rock. Pour a large spoonful of sand and a large spoonful of gravel in a cup. Fill the other cup 1 cm full of water. Add 5 spoonfuls of sugar and stir until it is all dissolved. Slowly pour some sugar water into the sand and gravel until it is all moistened. Pour off any extra water. Let it dry overnight. Then over a piece of paper, carefully tear the cup off. Let the "rock" harden for 2 days. Study your sedimentary "rock." How is it like a real rock? How is it different?

Metamorphic Rocks

Metamorphic (met´ə môr´ fik) rocks are formed when heat and pressure change other rocks. You observed how this works in the Explore Activity on pages 38–39. Any kind of rock, igneous, sedimentary, or metamorphic, can be changed in this way.

This cliff is made of slate, another metamorphic rock. Slate looks like a stack of thin, flat rocks. Some chalkboards are made from a large, thin piece of slate.

Granite

Heat and pressure change granite, an igneous rock, into gneiss (nīs). Does this rock look like the "rock" you made in the Explore Activity?

Gneiss

The Rock Cycle

The ground beneath your feet is a very busy place. Rocks are constantly made, changed, and broken down. They are moved around. They are pushed up from deep inside Earth. They are also forced far underground. Although most of these things happen very slowly, over millions of years, rocks are changed a lot. Where does all of this change take place?

All types of rocks can be changed. What happens to a certain rock depends on where the rock is.

Weathering and erosion take place at and close to the surface of Earth. The pieces of rocks are stuck together to make sedimentary rocks.

Sedimentary Rock

Igneous Rock

Metamorphic Rock

Heat from inside Earth melts rocks. As the melted rock material rises to the surface, it slowly cools to make igneous rocks.

Layers of rocks get pushed deeper into Earth. As they are squeezed and heated, they change to metamorphic rocks.

As rocks are changed, a kind of cycle is followed. A **cycle** (sī´ kəl) is a series of things that happen over and over. The **rock cycle** is a constant series of changes that happen to rocks. Weathering, erosion, melting, cooling, heating, and pressure keep this cycle going.

Sedimentary Rock

When a new kind of rock is formed, it can be changed again by any of the processes, depending where the rock is.

Weathering and Erosion

Igneous Sedimentary Metamorphic Rocks

Any rock, depending where it is, can be changed by weathering and erosion, melting and cooling, or heat and pressure.

Metamorphic Rock

Melting and Cooling

Heat and Pressure

Igneous Rock

Minds On! The path a rock takes depends on where the rock is on Earth. There is no certain order of changes. Look at the diagram. Imagine you are a rock. Starting as one type, what kinds of rocks can you be changed into? In your *Activity Log* on page 18, record the rocks you could become. What processes change you into each of those rocks? ●

Copying Rock Processes

People have found many uses for the processes that form rocks. Although most rocks take a long time to form, we can copy these processes and speed them up.

Bricks and pottery are made from clay and other materials. People make them the same way metamorphic rocks are formed. Bricks and pottery must be baked at very high temperatures to make them strong enough to use.

Concrete is made in a way similar to natural sedimentary rocks. It is a mixture of stones, water, and cement. When it dries, it becomes hard. Did you know sidewalks were made of concrete?

Social Studies Link

Built To Last

What are the houses and buildings in your neighborhood made of? There are many reasons people use wood, bricks, or rocks to make a building. Some walls made of rocks, like those built in Zimbabwe, have lasted thousands of years. Look at the houses and buildings in your neighborhood. How many are made of rock or brick? How many are made of wood? Record your observations in your *Activity Log* on page 19. What material is used the most? Why do you think that material was chosen?

Did you know that glass is made the same way as igneous rocks? In fact, it is very similar to the natural rock obsidian. Pure sand is melted at very high temperatures. Then it is cooled quickly to make glass. This artist needs to work quickly to form the glass in the shape he needs before it cools.

Sum It Up

You are standing on a busy rock "factory!" Rocks are being made, broken down, and remade all over Earth. This factory forms igneous, sedimentary, and metamorphic rocks differently. How it changes the three kinds of rocks is called the rock cycle.

Critical Thinking

1. Explain what would have to happen for a sedimentary rock to become an igneous rock.

2. How is the rock cycle different from the cycle of a washing machine?

3. Is a rock that you find in a stream more likely to become a sedimentary or an igneous rock? Why?

47

How Does Land Form and Change?

All kinds of interesting features cover the surface of Earth. Jagged mountain peaks, rounded foothills, and soft, sandy beaches decorate Earth's landscape. Why are these things here? Will they always be around?

A sand dune

A sea arch

Devils Tower

A land arch

A long arch called Landscape Arch joins two rocky cliffs in Utah. Devils Tower is a rock that stands 260 meters (865 feet) tall in Wyoming. Hills of sand, some nearly 180 meters (600 feet) high, cover the land at the Great Sand Dunes National Monument in Colorado. Many unusual features are found on Earth. How did they form?

Minds On! Look at the pictures of unusual rock formations. How do you think they were formed? Have they always looked like that? Write your ideas in your *Activity Log* on page 20.

Activity!

Water Power!

If water can change a rock, can it change a mountain or an entire continent? In this activity, you will construct a model from moist sand, gravel, and dirt. You will explore the effect water has on your model.

What You Need

Activity Log pages 21-22

sand

water

small gravel

dirt

2 paper cups

book

pencil

deep tray

What To Do

1 With your group, layer the gravel, sand, and dirt at one end of the tray. Smooth its surface. Leave the other end empty to collect water. Carefully moisten the sand until it is wet.

2 Place a book under the end of the tray with the sand. Draw a picture of this in your *Activity Log.*

3 Use the tip of a pencil to poke one small hole in the bottom of one paper cup.

4 Hold the cup with the hole above the sand. Fill it with water using the other cup. Watch the sand carefully while the water drains onto it. Watch what is happening to both the water and the sand.

5 After the water has stopped flowing, draw a picture of its new form and record your observations in your *Activity Log.*

What Happened?

1. How did the pile change?
2. What caused these changes?

What Now?

1. Suppose you raised the end higher with another book. How would this change what happens in the model? Predict first. Then reshape the pile and try it again. Compare the results.

2. If the paper cup had a bigger hole in it, how would that change your results? Try it and see.

3. How could water change rocks and land on Earth?

EXPLORE

Earth Changes

Water has a powerful part in shaping what the surface of Earth looks like. Not only can it break apart rocks, it can carry them away, too. In the activity you saw how "rain" carried away the sand and dirt, dumping it somewhere else. In a short time, the water changed the shape of your landscape.

Scientists say the Grand Canyon in Arizona was formed by many things that happened over millions of years. Rivers, seas, and deserts formed layers of sedimentary rock over very old igneous and metamorphic rocks.

Then the area was pushed up to make a plateau. A **plateau** (pla tō´) is a flat place that's raised up from the area around it. The carving by the river and weathering of the exposed layers of rock have continued to shape this unique landform.

Language Arts Link

Legends

There are many ways to explain how things like the Grand Canyon and mountains were formed. Ancient peoples from all over the world used stories to explain how these things happened. Some stories explained that these features were the result of battles between gods, animals, or people. Other stories involved heroes or heroines who did a great task to prove their love for one another. With two other people, make up a legend to explain how the Grand Canyon formed. Draw pictures to help tell your story. Share your legend with the class.

Features such as canyons, mountains, plateaus, plains, and islands are called **landforms**. The processes of the rock cycle not only change rocks, but they also create the landforms around us.

One way landforms are changed is by deposition (dep´ə zish´ ən) of rock parts. **Deposition** *happens when running water, ice, or wind slows down and drops many of the rock pieces being carried. Look at these pictures to see how deposition can form a river delta. Did you see this happen in the Explore Activity?*

Most mountains form by a combination of processes. Earth's surface is cracked, pushed, and bent. Lava pours out from deep underground. Before a mountain is finished forming, other processes like weathering and erosion begin to break it down.

Formation of a river delta

53

Slow Changes

Usually, we do not notice the changes in Earth's landforms because they take place over a long time. The Appalachian Mountains are very old. They began to form more than 400 million years ago! When change happens over that much time, it's no surprise you don't notice it!

After hundreds of years, the section of the Snake River shown in the photo might look like this. ▶

This is what the Snake River looks like now.

The Himalaya Mountains in central Asia are some of the tallest mountains in the world. They are slowly growing about two centimeters every year.

Measuring Mountains and Molehills

How do people know that a mountain is getting taller or being worn down? They measure it! But you couldn't just use a meter stick, could you? To measure how high mountains and other things are, different tools are used.

Scientists have used lasers to measure such large distances. More recently satellites circling Earth have been used.

With these tools, scientists can measure mountains to the closest centimeter! By comparing several measurements of a mountain over many years, they can observe if the mountain is getting bigger or smaller.

Fast Changes

Some landforms change quickly. Waves crash on beaches, moving sand out to sea. The ocean currents then deposit the sand somewhere else. Heavy storms and floods move rocks and soil, changing the shape of the land. Earthquakes or volcanoes can change Earth's surface in just a few minutes.

Rockslides send rocks down a mountainside or cliff in seconds.

56

Mudslides *like this one move large amounts of very wet mud down a mountain.*

Many areas with unusual landforms have been set aside to protect them. The Grand Canyon is a national park. The world's tallest mountain, Mount Everest, is protected by the government of Nepal (nə pôl´). Japan has put a lot of work into protecting Mount Fuji (fü´ jē). What do you think might have happened to these unusual landforms if they were not set aside as national parks and monuments?

Changing Landforms Change Your World

Over time, the results of weathering, erosion, and deposition can cause problems for people. Rivers can slowly erode fields and yards. Mudslides often destroy houses. Buildings and highways can collapse during earthquakes. Lava and ash from volcanoes can endanger people's lives, too.

TRY THIS

Activity!

Is Your School Yard Changing?

What You Need
Activity Log page 23

Take a mini field trip around the school yard. Look for small examples of erosion and deposition. Go out after a rain shower or after a very windy day. What evidence can you see of erosion, weathering, or deposition? Record your observations in your *Activity Log.* Which changes are caused by people? Which happen naturally?

Sometimes highways and the rocks under them are washed away.

People do all kinds of things to try to stop erosion. One way is to use plants. Plant roots hold soil in place. This helps stop the soil from being washed or blown away. By planting grass or other plants, people protect their land from erosion.

*In places where there aren't many plants, wind and rain are free to erode the soil. The wind blows it around, sometimes making huge piles of sand called **sand dunes** as on page 48. Almost as easily as the wind ruffles your hair, a windstorm can rearrange sand dunes.*

Sum It Up

Like many things, the surface of Earth is changing over time. The ice, water, and wind that change rocks can also change mountains, beaches, and other landforms. The changes can happen over several million years or several minutes. Mountains, rivers, and beaches look very different from the way they did long ago. And, they will keep changing for years to come.

Critical Thinking

1. Some people have built houses along the seashore. What kinds of problems do you think they might have from weathering and erosion?

2. Does wind, water, or ice do the most weathering and erosion in a desert? Why?

3. If you took a photograph of a mountain, would it look the same in one million years? How might it change?

What Else Is Beneath Your Feet?

You walk on it. You run on it. Your school is built on it. But have you ever thought about what it is you're living on? You are probably very familiar with the ground right under your feet. You can see soil and probably some rocks. In most places, if you dig a hole, you find more of the same thing. Have you ever wondered what you would find if you could keep digging? What would you find Earth is made of? Is it solid rock? Is it hollow? Would you eventually end up on the other side of the world?

Minds On! What do you think Earth is made of? Discuss with the rest of your class what you think is inside Earth. •

A view of Earth from space

If you want to try digging a hole through Earth, you'd better plan on spending a lot of time! The deepest scientists have dug so far is just over twelve km. (about 7.5 miles).

60

Could You Ever? Dig a Hole to China

People have always been curious about what Earth is made of. Scientists want to know, too! In the book, *Could You Ever? Dig a Hole to China*, Dr. David Darling describes some of the things you might find far beneath your feet. Read and discover what scientists have found out about what Earth is made of.

After reading this book, discuss in a small group if it's possible to dig a hole through Earth. What problems would you have? What things might you find?

The rocks, soil, and water you see when you look at Earth are just part of what makes up this planet. Between the outer layer we share with other living things and Earth's center lie about 6,400 kilometers (about 4,000 miles) of other materials. Imagine Earth as a giant apple. All the rocks and landforms are located within the peel.

Although it is small compared to the rest of Earth, the outer layer is very interesting. Let's take a look at this layer right beneath your feet.

Most of Earth's land is covered with the pieces of rocks and minerals made by weathering. When combined with water, air, and things that were once living, it makes soil.

As new rocks are made, new layers are formed. Sedimentary rocks form slowly at the bottoms of oceans. Lava may ooze from a volcano and cool to form new igneous rocks. Heat and pressure from inside Earth may change some rocks to metamorphic rocks.

Beneath this are layers and layers of different kinds of rocks. These layers can be up to 40 kilometers (25 miles) thick.

Activity!

Learning From a Rock

What You Need

favorite rock from rock collection, book about rocks, *Activity Log* page 24

There are many reasons why you picked your favorite rock. But did you know you can learn things from your rock? Look in a book about rocks and use it to help you figure out what kind of rock you have. Is it an igneous, metamorphic, or sedimentary rock? Has it always been that kind of rock? In your ***Activity Log,*** tell the life story of your rock. Describe where and how it formed. What landforms was it part of? What processes of the rock cycle have changed it?

Underneath all of these layers of rocks lies a thick layer of rock material. It is a very hot layer of rocks that is more than 2,800 kilometers (about 1,800 miles) thick.

Deeper inside Earth is a layer of melted metal. This liquid layer surrounds the center of Earth, which is a solid ball of metal.

As you look at Earth, maybe now you will see it differently. The next time you pick up a rock, take some time to look at it. Try to see different minerals that might be in it. Think about the changes it has been through. And think about how you have just changed Earth, ever so slightly, by picking it up!

GLOSSARY

Use the pronunciation key below to help you decode, or read, the pronunciations.

Pronunciation Key

a	at, bad	d	dear, soda, bad
ā	ape, pain, day, break	f	five, defend, leaf, off, cough, elephant
ä	father, car, heart	g	game, ago, fog, egg
âr	care, pair, bear, their, where	h	hat, ahead
e	end, pet, said, heaven, friend	hw	white, whether, which
ē	equal, me, feet, team, piece, key	j	joke, enjoy, gem, page, edge
i	it, big, English, hymn	k	kite, bakery, seek, tack, cat
ī	ice, fine, lie, my	l	lid, sailor, feel, ball, allow
îr	ear, deer, here, pierce	m	man, family, dream
o	odd, hot, watch	n	not, final, pan, knife
ō	old, oat, toe, low	ng	long, singer, pink
ô	coffee, all, taught, law, fought	p	pail, repair, soap, happy
ôr	order, fork, horse, story, pour	r	ride, parent, wear, more, marry
oi	oil, toy	s	sit, aside, pets, cent, pass
ou	out, now	sh	shoe, washer, fish mission, nation
u	up, mud, love, double	t	tag, pretend, fat, button, dressed
ū	use, mule, cue, feud, few	th	thin, panther, both
ü	rule, true, food	th	this, mother, smooth
ů	put, wood, should	v	very, favor, wave
ûr	burn, hurry, term, bird, word, courage	w	wet, weather, reward
ə	about, taken, pencil, lemon, circus	y	yes, onion
b	bat, above, job	z	zoo, lazy, jazz, rose, dogs, houses
ch	chin, such, match	zh	vision, treasure, seizure

asbestos (as bes´təs) a grayish-white mineral that will not allow heat to travel through it very well

canyon (kan´ yən) a deep valley with steep sides, usually with a stream running through it

chemical weathering (kem´i kəl · weth´ər´ ing) the changing of chemicals that make up minerals

crystal (kris´təl) a repeating pattern of particles that make up minerals

cycle (sī kəl) a series of events that happen over and over again

delta (del´ tə) an area of land that is formed by the deposition of sand, pebbles, and other fine rock particles where a river empties into a lake or ocean

deposition (dep´ə zish´ən) the process of laying down, or dropping rocks and minerals when running water, ice, or wind slows down

dissolve (di zolv´) to cause a solid or gas to mix in with a liquid until it can no longer be seen

erosion (i rō´zhen) the process of carrying away rocks and minerals by wind, water, ice, or sliding

igneous (ig´nē əs) a type of rock formed from the cooling of melted rock material

landform (land´form) a feature on the surface of Earth such as canyons, mountains, plateaus, plains, and islands. These can be changed by the processes of erosion in the rock cycle.

metamorphic (met´ə môr´fik) a type of rock formed when heat and pressure change other rocks

mineral (min´ər əl) a naturally-formed solid that has a definite structure inside

mudslide (mud´slīd) a movement of large amounts of wet mud down the slope of a mountain or hill

plateau (pla tō´) an area of flat land that's raised up from the area around it

property (prop´ər tē) a characteristic of something. Minerals have different properties such as color, hardness and shape.

rock (rok) a mixture of one or more minerals

rock cycle (rok · sī´ kəl) a constant series of changes that happens to rocks—weathering, erosion, deposition, melting, cooling, heating, and pressure keep this cycle going

rockslide (rok´slīd) a rapid movement of many rocks down the slope of a mountain or hill

sand dune (sand · dün) a large mound or hill of sand deposited by wind

sedimentary (sed´ə men´tə rē) a type of rock that is made from the weathered pieces of rocks which have been transported, deposited and stuck together

soil (soil) a combination of weathered rocks and minerals, dead plants and animals, water, and air

weathering (weth´ər´ing) the process of wind, water, or ice breaking rock into smaller pieces, and the chemical changes occurring to minerals and rocks

INDEX

African people, 8, 27
Anasazi people, 9
Appalachian Mountains, 54
Asbestos, 25

Baylor, Byrd, 10
Big Rock, The (Hiscock), 11
Book reviews, 10-11
Breaking patterns, 21
Bricks, 46
Building materials, *act.*, 46

Calcite, 23
Canyons, 52
Caves, 32
Chalk, 23, 42
Chemical weathering, 32; *act.*, 32
Clay, 24
Cleopatra's Needle, *illus.*, 30
Cliff–dwelling people, 9
Climate, 30-31
Color, of minerals, 20, *act.*, 20; *illus.*, 20-21
Concrete, 46
Coquina, *illus.*, 42
Could You Ever? Dig a Hole to China (Darling) 11, 61

Crystals, 41
Cycles, 45

Darling, Dr. David, 11, 61
Deposition, 53; *act.*, 50-51
Devils Tower, *illus.*, 49
Diamonds, 21, 23
Dissolving, of minerals, 32
Dust storms, *illus.*, 59

Earth, *illus.*, 60, 62-63; changes to, 52-59; composition, 60-63; layers, 62-63
Egyptian people, 9
Erosion, 31, 58, 59
Everest, Mount, 57
Everybody Needs a Rock (Baylor), 10

Feldspar, *illus.*, 16
Flint, 8
Fuji, Mount, 57

Geography From A to Z (Knowlton), 11
Glass making, 47
Gneiss, *illus.*, 37, 43
Gold rush, 19
Grand Canyon, 57; *illus.*, 52-53

Granite, *illus.*, 16, 41, 43
Graphite, 22, 23
Great Sand Dunes National Monument, 49
Great Wall of China, *illus.*, 8-9
Great Zimbabwe, 27; *illus.*, 26

Half Dome, *illus.*, 6-7
Halite, 18
Hardness, 18-19, 22-23; *act.*, 18
Heat, rock changes by, 43, 44
Himalaya Mountains, *illus.*, 55
Hiscock, Bruce, 11

Ice, rock changes by, 30, 31; *act.*, 28-29
Igneous rocks, 40-41, 44, 47; *illus.*, 40-41, 44, 45

Jewelry makers, 41

Knowlton, Jack, 11

Landforms, changes to, 48-59; *act.*, 58; formation, 48-59; protection, 57

Land arch, *illus.*, 49
Lava, *illus.*, 40
Legends, 52
Limestone, 42

Metamorphic rocks, 43, 44; *illus.*, 44, 45
Mica, *illus.*, 16
Miller, Valerie, 41
Minerals, 16; breaking patterns, 21; color, 20; *act.*, 20; *illus.*, 20-21; dissolved, 32; hardness, 18-19, 22-23; *act.*, 18; health hazards, 25; properties, 17-21; *act.*, 18; shininess, *act.*, 20; in soils, 33; uses for, 22-25; weathering, 34-35
Modeling clay, 24
Monument Valley, *illus.*, 36
Mountains, changes to, 54-55; formation, 53; measurement, 55
Mudslides, *illus.*, 57

Native American people, 9, 41

Obsidian, 41, 47

Peters, Lisa Westberg, 11
Plateaus, 52
Pollution, weathering and, 35

Potholes, 34
Pottery, 24, 46
Pressure, rock changes by, 43; *act.*, 38-39
Properties, minerals, 17-21; *act.*, 18
Pyramids, 9
Pyrite, 19

Quartz, 18; *illus.*, 17

Rain, rock changes by, 30,
River delta, *illus.*, 53
Roads, weather damage, 34
Rock collections, *act.*, 7, 17, 63
Rock cycles, 44-45, 53; *act.*, 45; *illus.*, 44-45
Rock formations, *act.*, 49; *illus.*, 49
Rocks, as building materials, *act.*, 46; changes in, 26-35; *act.*, 28-29, 31, 32, 33, 34; *illus.*, 26-27, 34, 35; composition, 12-25; *act.*, 14-15; description, *act.*, 7, 63; formation, 36-47; *act.*, 38-39; as tools, 8-9; under pressure, 43; *act.*, 38-39; uses for, 8-9, 13, 41; weathering, 30-35; *act.*, 32, 33, 34
Rockslides, *illus.*, 56

Salt, 18

Sand dunes, 59; *illus.*, 48
Sandblasting, 19
Sandpaper, 19
Sandstone, *illus.*, 37
Sedimentary rocks, 42, 44; *act.*, 43; *illus.*, 37
Shininess, minerals, *act.*, 20
Sidewalks, 35
Snake River, *illus.*, 54
Soil, formation, 33; *act.*, 33; *illus.*, 33; minerals in, 33
Stone Age people, 8-9
Stones, *See* Rocks
Sun, the Wind and the Rain, The (Peters), 11

Volcanoes, *illus.*, 37, 40

Water, landform changes by, 52; *act.*, 50-51; rock changes by, *act.*, 28-29, 30, 31
Weathering, 30-35; *act.*, 32, 33, 34; *illus.*, 30-35
White Cliffs of Dover, *illus.*, 42
Wind, rock changes by, 31

Yosemite National Park, *illus.*, 6-7

Zimbabwe, 27; *illus.*, 26

CREDITS